¡ES MI CUMPLEAÑOS!/ IT'S MY BIRTHDAY!

By Tina Benjamin   Traducido por Charlotte Bockman

 Gareth Stevens
PUBLISHING

Please visit our website, www.garethstevens.com. For a free color catalog of all our high-quality books, call toll free 1-800-542-2595 or fax 1-877-542-2596.

Library of Congress Cataloging-in-Publication Data

Benjamin, Tina.
It's my birthday = ¡Es mi cumpleaños! / by Tina Benjamin.
    pages cm. — (Inside my world = Mi Mundo)
Parallel title: Mi Mundo.
In English and Spanish.
Includes index.
ISBN 978-1-4824-2356-3 (library binding)
1. Birthdays — Juvenile literature. 2. Birthday parties — Juvenile literature. I. Benjamin, Tina. II. Title.
GT2430.B46 2015
392—d23

First Edition

Published in 2015 by
Gareth Stevens Publishing
111 East 14th Street, Suite 349
New York, NY 10003

Copyright © 2015 Gareth Stevens Publishing

Editor: Nathalie Beullens-Maoui
Designer: Sarah Liddell
Spanish Translation: Charlotte Bockman

Photo credits: Cover, p. 1 Pinkcandy/Shutterstock.com; p. 5 Pressmaster/Shutterstock.com; pp. 7, 19, 24 (balloons) Africa Studio/Shutterstock.com; pp. 9, 11, 15, 17, 19, 21, 23, 24 (soccer ball) Hurst Photo/Shutterstock.com; pp. 13, 24 (candles) tobkatrina/Shutterstock.com.

Printed in the United States of America

CPSIA compliance information: Batch #CW15GS: For further information contact Gareth Stevens, New York, New York at 1-800-542-2595.

Contenido

- -

Contents

¡Voy a tener una fiesta
de cumpleaños!

I am having
a birthday party!

5

Hay muchos globos.
Los globos amarillos
son mis favoritos.

We have lots
of balloons.
Yellow balloons are
my favorite.

¡Invité a todos
mis amigos!

I invited all my friends!

Mi mamá me hizo
un pastel.

My mom made me
a cake.

Le pusimos velitas.

We put candles on it.

13

¡Pido un deseo!
Soplo las velitas.

I make a wish!
I blow out the candles.

¡El pastel está muy rico!

The cake tastes
really good!

Recibí muchos regalos.

I got lots of presents.

19

Mi hermano me regaló
una pelota de fútbol.

My brother got me
a soccer ball.

Jugamos con ella
en el jardín.

We play with it
in the yard.

Palabras que debes saber/ Words to Know

(los) globos/
balloon

(las) velitas/
candles

(la) pelota de fútbol/
soccer ball

Índice/Index

24